Love, Mutual Assistance and "the World of Great Harmony"

By Louis TW Lan

ISBN: 9798468239346

DEDICATION

For brothers and sisters, who love ourselves and the earth,

Whether you believe in the Creator [Note 1] or not, please be sure to understand the upcoming content of avoiding crises/death and welcoming happiness as follow.

In recent years, a series of natural disasters and epidemic infectious diseases including the COVID-19 virus and a series of variant viruses are just small warnings to human beings. In the future, larger natural disasters and deadly epidemic infectious diseases will follow. If we still don't love and help each other, the intensive natural disasters, deadly epidemic diseases, wars caused by selfishness and hatred then a further nuclear war will completely destroy the earth and all human beings. We, human beings, are rational because we have ideals, and we are great because we practice ideals. After understanding the content of this book, we work together to abandon the destruction of the earth and all human beings due to selfishness, hatred, wars leading a further nuclear war, and achieve "the World of Great Harmony" [Note 2] with love, mutual assistance, peace and happiness!

CONTENTS

1 THE ESSENCE OF RELIGIONS AND THE MEANING OF LOVE

"Money talks." Money is certainly needed. However the most important thing is not money and material desires, but improvement of spirituality. The existence of money and material in a person's life is only around 80 years, but the spirituality is eternal. The eighty years of the human body is for the spiritual experience and spiritual improvement. Compared with the eternal spirituality, money and material are only short-lived, and they are not taken away when death. If you violate the law due to coveting other people's money and material, or even infringe upon others, not only will the spirituality in this life unable to improve, but the spiritual experience of this life will be wasted, and it will even sink down. The reverence for the God and essence of love is the same in all major religions around the world. This book does not discuss individual religions, but reveals the only direction for human beings. Please read the following content, the crises/destruction or happiness of human beings depends on our choice. **The ultimate goal of the world's major religions at the beginning is to enhance moral level and spirituality, and the essence of each religion and intersection is love , which is simple, direct and pure. After that, the religions have been added with red tape from spread word of mouth and some other needs or purposes. Even some people with ulterior ambitions extended these red tape to resort to violence, aggression against others, and even caused religious wars. Numerous religious wars have caused more than tens of millions of deaths and injuries. Nowadays some people carry out planned**

and undifferentiated terrorist attacks because of the personal extreme thought generated from some red tape of a certain religion. It is very extreme and runs counter to the Creator and the original intents of the religions. How can we not correct such a wrong behavior that is drifting away? It is recommended to simplify the red tape of the religions, and gradually focus on love and mutual assistance to reach the improvement of moral level and spirituality. **Love is the eternal and worry-free way of human beings.** Ten Commandments of Judaism, Catholicism and Christianity, the Five Merits of Islam, the Eternal Responsibility of Hinduism, the Five Precepts and Ten Good Karma of Buddhism are with love. The ultimate goal of the major religions in the world is the ascension of moral levels and spirituality, and the essence and intersection is love. "Leviticus 19:18 of Judaism" indicated "You shall not take vengeance or bear a grudge against your kinsfolk. Love your neighbor as yourself: I am the Lord". "Matthew 7:12" of the New Testament indicated "Do to others what you want them to do to you. This is the

3

meaning of the law of Moses and the teaching of the prophets". The prophet Muhammad of Islam said that "As you would have people do to you, do to them; and what you dislike to be done to you, don't do to them." "Brihaspati, Mahabharata 13.113.8" of Hinduism indicated "One should never do that to another which one regards as injurious to one's own self. This, in brief, is the rule of dharma. Other behavior is due to selfish desires." and also "By making dharma your main focus, treat others as you treat yourself.". "Dhammapada 10. Violence" of Buddhism indicated "One who, while himself seeking happiness, oppresses with violence other beings who also desire happiness, will not attain happiness hereafter.".

The reverence for the God and essence of love is the same in all major religions around the world

Confucianism is the mainstream thought of Chinese culture. Confucius and Mencius are the representatives of Confucianism. Confucianism believes that benevolence/love is the foundation and the most fundamental moral starting point of human beings. Confucius said: "Young people should be filial to their parents, be friendly to brothers and sisters, respect teachers, be serious and honest, show love, and be close to people with lofty ideals. If you can do this, you can engage in academic research." Mencius said: "Benevolent people are people full of love; Polite people respect others. He who loves others, others love him. He who respects others, others respect him." When the collective consciousness of human beings in the world has gradually transformed from selfishness to 100% love, it is "the World of Great Harmony". Knowing the following, if we can choose love, mutual assistance, harmony, peace and happiness, who will continue to choose hatred, fear, wars and misery?

All spirituality with love, harmony and peace

Both Isaac Newton and Albert Einstein made great contributions to scientific research. Besides, in their later years, they studied the final answers to questions about the universe, they both believed that the universe is a masterpiece of the God (the Creator). Isaac Newton's three laws of motion established the mechanical foundation of physics, enabling us to understand the laws of the development of the universe. Although he understood the movement of the world, he firmly believed in the existence of the God (the Creator) when studying why the universe moves. The scientist Albert Einstein admired most was Isaac Newton. Albert had the same view as Isaac. [Note 3] He also believed that the universe is a masterpiece of the God (the Creator). Now human beings know that the universe was born because of the Big Bang. How was the universe before the Big Bang? How did the Big Bang happen? Why did the Big Bang form such a perfect universe? Why do the stars maintain such an ideal state for billions of years? Why is there no large-scale collision of stars that further caused the collision of clusters of gravitational chains and eventually the universe collapsed? The sun continues to move in the universe with the eight planets and the entire solar system. The entire solar system is wrapped in a huge protective system formed by the solar wind, that is, the heliosphere. Imagine that when the sun and all its planets are moving at a very high speed of about 250 kilometers per second in the Milky Way, the sun, the planets and the asteroid belt of the Kuiper belt can magically rotate and revolve in systems without colliding with each other or deviating from their original tracks. The heliosphere keeps most harmful cosmic rays and other substances out of the solar system and protects the earth and all lives on the earth.

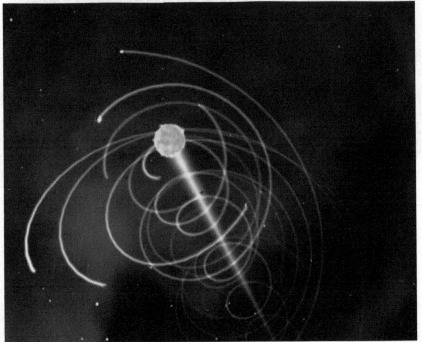

Imagine that when the sun and all its planets are moving at a very high speed of about 250 kilometers per second in the Milky Way, the sun, the planets and the asteroid belt of the

Kuiper belt can magically rotate and revolve in systems without colliding with each other or deviating from their original tracks, while the solar system is protected by the heliosphere.

Who can create this perfect universe besides the Creator?

Who is able to create this perfect universe besides the Creator? Countless lives come from the love of the Creator, and this love is spiritual love. Mankind has a higher self and an ego. The higher self is love, mutual assistance, and sharing while the ego is desire, hatred and selfishness.　　Whether you believe in the Creator or not, you know that the higher self is the spirit of love, mutual assistance, and sharing.　The ego is desire, hatred and selfishness. Chinese "Three Character Classic (Chinese:三字經)" indicates "At the beginning of human beings, human nature is good.". This good mentioned here is kindness, which is the higher self and is also love, mutual assistance, and sharing.　In addition, that China's Xunzi (Chinese:荀子) said "Human nature is evil" is biased.　It should be that human nature is "selfish".　This "selfish" is the ego, which is desire, hatred and selfishness.　　Excessive selfishness will generate evil, then cause crimes. Therefore, everyone have a higher self and an ego.　That "Human nature is good" is the higher self while that "Human nature is also selfish" is the ego.

Higher Self	Ego
Love	Hatred
Mutual Assistance	Selfishness
Sharing	Desire

Forgiveness	Punishment
Courage	Fear
Abundance	Poverty
Harmony	Struggle
Peace	War
Happiness	Misery

The difference between Higher Self and Ego

Human beings are spiritual, and human bodies are material. Without spirituality, the body is just a corpse. Anyone who is confused by material desires will be trapped by the ego, and will always want to satisfy different desires, but forgets his spiritual love, and finally sinks into the struggle for material desires, which is extremely painful. Even if a very small number of people are lucky enough to become billionaires, they fear that their property will be stolen and that they and their family will be kidnapped and killed due to property. They are fearful and uneasy at all time. We need to elevate our moral level and restore spiritual love, rather than becoming a slave to material things. Let us return to love and mutual assistance in order to enter the ideal state of everyone: "the World of Great Harmony".

Should we choose selfishness, hatred and struggle of the ego then results in wars causing a nuclear war that leads to the destruction of the earth and all human beings? Or should we choose love, mutual assistance, and peace of higher self and then the earth becomes "the World of Great Harmony"? This answer is very simple.

The transparent systems and solutions for "Politics and Systems" and "Food, Clothing, Housing, Transportation, Education, and entertainment" are detailed in the following chapters. "Politics and Institutions" are detailed in "3. The earth forming a single United Nations in accordance with the new United Nations Constitution" and "6. UN soldiers and weapons not to deal with human beings unless armed insurgent groups.". "Food, clothing and transportation" are detailed in "5. Basic food/clothing and free from fear", "7. Sharing resources and cooperation with each other" and "9. Greenhouse crops and optimized food". "Housing" is detailed in "5. Basic food/clothing and free from fear " and "7. Sharing resources and cooperation with each other". "Education and entertainment" are detailed in "4. Achieving love and mutual assistance through love education", "5. Basic food/clothing and free from fear " and "9. Greenhouse crops and optimized food". Environmental protection is detailed in "8. Environmental protection and love for the earth".

Before the beginning of the twentieth century, there was no international standard for musical pitch, and most people applied pitch lower than A=440 hertz (Hz). The opera master, Giuseppe Verdic, praised A=432 Hz, and believed that this is the standard tone to perfectly show the charm of his opera. In addition, most musicians such as Johann Sebastian Bach, Wolfgang Amadeus Mozart, Ludwig van Beethoven also applied the pitch lower than A=440 Hz to compose their music. The Nazis set the musical pitch at A=440 Hz according to their needs, and advocated this setting. In year 1953, the International Organization for Standardization (ISO) also uniformly set the pitch at A=440 Hz, then most of the world's music has been adjusted to A=440 Hz accordingly. Many musicians recently played music at A=432 Hz and found that the sand oscillation pattern was more orderly and beautiful than that at A=440 Hz, and the water sound vibration was also more orderly and beautiful at A=432 Hz. Since around 70% of the human body is water, they recommend applying A=432 Hz as the musical pitch. Please refer to the following figure [Note 4], which shows that water vibrates more peacefully and regularly when A=432 Hz than when A=440 Hz. Even scientists such as Nikola Tesla and Albert Einstein spoke of the importance of viewing everything in terms of vibration, energy, and frequency. **Nikola Tesla said "If you want to find the secrets of the universe, think in terms of energy, frequency and vibration."** Please also refer to the following chart of the examples of relationship between 432 and the universe. **432 reveals the important code of the universe and is the golden figure of the universe.** 432 Hz is the most coordinated frequency with the universe. It is said that 432 Hz vibrates with the universe's golden mean, Phi, and unifies the properties of light, time, space, matter, gravity, and magnetism with biology, the DNA code, and consciousness. When our atoms and DNA start to resonate in harmony with the spiraling pattern of nature, our sense of connection to nature is said to be magnified. The number 432 is also reflected in ratios of the sun, the earth, and the moon, as well as the procession of the equinoxes, the Great Pyramid of Egypt, Stonehenge, and the Sri Yantra, among many other sacred sites [Note 4]. The music at A=432 Hz sounds more peaceful, elegant, warm and enlightening, and it is also loved by most musicians while the current A=440 Hz music sounds more impulsive, sharp, saturated, disturbing and does not reconcile with the melody of the universe. **It is recommended to adopt the suggestions of most musicians and change the standard pitch from A=440 Hz to A=432 Hz, which** makes music more peaceful, elegant, warm and enlightening. It's also to set the most harmonious music to reconcile with the melody of the universe. The peaceful, elegant, warm and enlightening music of A=432 Hz helps human beings to enhance mutual love, mutual assistance, harmony and peace then replaces the impulsive, disturbing and impatient music at A=440 Hz that leads to selfishness and combativeness.

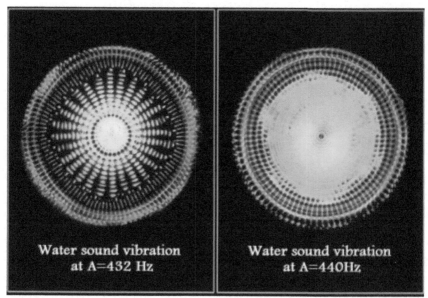

Water sound vibration at A=432 Hz versus 440 Hz
[Note 4]

Number	432	Multiples of 432	108	Multiples of 108	Remark
25920	432	60	108	240	The time for the solar system to make one revolution in the Milky Way is around 25,920 years (60 times 432)
864000	432	2000	108	8000	The diameter of the sun is around 864,000 miles (2,000 times 432)
108	432	1/4	108	1	The diameter of the sun is around 108 times the diameter of the earth (a quarter of 432)
108	432	1/4	108	1	The distance between the sun and the earth is around 108 times the diameter of the sun (a quarter of 432)
108	432	1/4	108	1	The distance between the moon and the earth is around 108 times the diameter of the moon (a quarter of 432)
86400	432	200	108	800	The earth's rotation (one day) is around 86400 seconds (200 times 432)
4320	432	10	108	40	Mars is around 4,320 miles in diameter (10 times 432)
86400	432	200	108	800	Jupiter is around 86,400 miles in diameter (200 times 432)
4320	432	10	108	40	Jupiter's orbital period is around 4320 days (10 times 432)

Examples of 432 relationship with the Universe

The perimeter of the Great Pyramid of Egypt multiplied by 43200 times is the circumference of the earth, and the height of the Great Pyramid multiplied by 43200 times is half the distance from the North Pole to the equator.

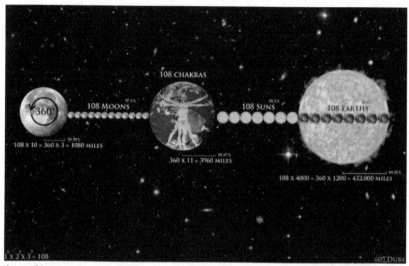

The diameter of the sun is approximately 864,000 miles (2,000 times 432)

The diameter of the sun is approximately 108 times the diameter of the earth (a quarter of 432)

The distance between the sun and the earth is approximately 108 times the diameter of the sun (a quarter of 432)

The distance between the moon and the earth is approximately 108 times the diameter of the moon (a quarter of 432) [Note 5]

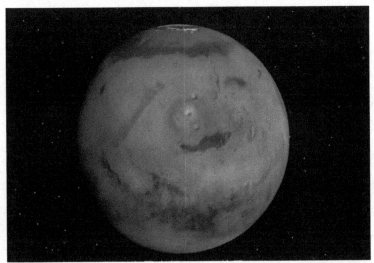

Mars is approximately 4,320 miles in diameter (10 times 432)

Jupiter is approximately 86,400 miles in diameter (200 times 432) and its orbital period is approximately 4,320 days (10 times 432).

The general wishes of the people on the earth are as follows:

- I wish to help many people.
- I want to be a policeman to maintain law/order and arrest gangsters.
- My target is to become a rich man with a lot of money.
- I hope that my career is real estate and I build many houses for the poor to live in.
- My goal is to be a president of a country.
- I wish to become a decorator and design many beautiful decorating houses for customers.
- I want to be an environmental fighter, protect the environment and love the earth.
- I wish to be a doctor and help patients.
- I want to be a teacher and educate students.
- I wish to be a successful entrepreneur.
- I wish to be a fashion designer to design beautiful clothes for customers.
- I want to be a driver and pick up passengers warmly.

- I wish to be a happy earth traveler to arrive happily and leave comfortably.
- I hope that my life is full of joy and love, even though I am on the green and embrace the sky.
- My goal is to be a scientist to invent and contribute to the world.
- I wish to rule the world.
- I wish to help the poor.
- I wish to be a good chef and provide good food to customers.
- My wish is to be an engineer to innovate machines/products for human beings' benefit.
- I hope that in my life, I have much money and less work, being close to home, sleeping until I wake up naturally.
- I hope my life is carefree, healthy, safe, prosperous and happy.

No matter which of the above is your wish, as long as the ideal of "the World of Great Harmony" with love and mutual assistance is achieved, your wish will be implemented. The content is detailed in the following ten chapters. If your wish is to be a national leader, you are the national leader in "the World of Great Harmony". In "the World of Great Harmony", democratic and free systems are implemented, and the general direction of the nation is decided by the people's vote. The people are the decision makers of the country so that you are the leader of the country. If your wish is to help many people, you will do so in "the World of Great Harmony". It's because all systems in "the World of Great Harmony" are transparent and fair, and everyone is taken care of for free and perfect. If your wish is to be a scientist to invent and contribute to the world, you can do so with relevant education as you wish to engage in the desired work and contribute to the world. If your desire is to be a happy earth traveler, who can arrive happily and leave comfortably, then you will be able to do what you want. In "the World of Great Harmony", employed men and women have ideal jobs, even if it is a very easy job. Both men and women of marriageable age can find suitable partners. The world and resources are shared by the public and all people. The systems are fair and transparent. All people have their own share, and have the rights to be free from fear, and with basic food, clothing and the related so that they are happy earth travelers that can arrive happily and leave comfortably.

If you ask "Can all the above wishes be realized?" The answer is "Yes" per the following content. We are the inhabitants of the earth and the messengers of love in the world. We reject hatred, excessive selfishness, fear, wars and misery but show love, mutual assistance, harmony, peace and happiness. This change is not out of reach, but just a short time. As long as we insist on love and mutual assistance, and establish fair, transparent and complete law and systems, everyone is well taken care of and lives happily and worry-free. When the collective consciousness of all human beings is love and mutual assistance, "the World of Great Harmony" can be achieved, and all the above wishes can be implemented.

2 ELIMINATING VIOLENCE AND WAR

At the beginning of human beings, human nature is "selfish" per ego. When selfishness gradually expands, acts of infringement on others cause crimes, such as robbing or stealing other people's property. When selfishness grows extremely, serious offenses against others cause serious crimes, such as murder, terrorist attacks, or war. We must respect the free will of individuals. We, human beings, are different from animals because we have ideals and the thought of love and mutual assistance to reform the earth to become "the World of Great Harmony." However, animals only compete each other, and there is no love and mutual assistance to become an ideal world of animals.

All crimes should be subject to judicial trial and correction, and prisons should still exist. Bullying of any age including children and young people must be prohibited and corrected. If it is illegal, it must be dealt with in accordance with the law. Do things for good even small, and do not do things for evil even small. Confucius said: "Administrated by government orders and criminal law, the people dare not commit crimes, but they are not ashamed of committing crimes. Guided by moral, benevolence and etiquette, the people will not only observe the etiquette, but also learn from a higher level of performance. Therefore, the people not only abide by the law, but also have more shame, can self-review, and learn from each other to improve moral." Due to the implementation of education and enlightenment, the moral and spirituality of all human beings will gradually improve, and the prisons will gradually decrease. We must eliminate all crimes, violence and wars, and improve the moral and spiritual level of all human beings.

History tells us how terrible war is. The death toll of the Anshi civil war of Tang Dynasty in China in the 8th century was about 13 million. The death toll of the Mongolian West Expedition and the Southern Expedition in the 13th century was about 50 million. The death toll of the civil war of the Golden Horde of the Mongolian Empire in the 14th century was about 15 million. The death toll of a series of civil wars of China's Qing army overthrew the Ming Dynasty in the 17th century was about 30 million. The death toll of the civil war of the White Lotus Uprising in China in the 18th century was about 16 million. The death toll of the Civil War of the Taiping Heavenly Kingdom in China in the 19th century was about 20 million. The death toll of the civil war of the Hui Uprising in China in the 19th century was about 12 million. The death toll of the Russian Civil War from 1917 to 1922 was about 11 million. The death toll of the First World War was about 35 million, and the death toll of the Second World War was about 70 million. Looking at the ten most deadly wars in the world, China had participated in as many as seven wars! The above ten wars caused the deaths of more than tens of millions of people, and the wounded are countless. [Note 6] The history of human beings is a series of wars. It can be seen the importance of eliminating violence and wars, especially the tens of thousands of nuclear weapons that may destroy the earth and all human beings are controlled in the hands of a few people currently.

We have no right to deliberately provoke wars due to selfishness, greed, and hatred, leading to nuclear wars to destroy the earth and all human beings

     Serious selfishness leads to wars, and the current powerful countries with nuclear bombs can cause the destruction of the earth and all human beings. However, the decision-making of this major fatal crises only rest in the hands of a very small number of persons among the seven billion people on the earth. Especially, the history of human beings is a series of wars. Furthermore, there are recently Middle East (Israel and Iran) crisis, the Indian Peninsula crisis, China-India territorial dispute crisis, Diaoyutai Islands (or Diaoyu Islands or Senkaku Islands) territorial dispute crisis, the South China Sea crisis, the Taiwan Strait crisis, the North Korea crisis, and the Eastern European crisis. The consequences of each crisis may lead to a serious nuclear war and the destruction of the earth and all human beings.

The crises may cause wars leading a nuclear war to destroy the earth and all human beings.

Due to the intention of any leader of a country with nuclear bombs to reverse the decline of the war or any misjudgment of the situation, a single button may trigger a nuclear war to destroy the earth and all human beings. The radiation, shock waves and radioactive materials produced by any nuclear war will cause destruction. At present, the explosive power of any neutron bomb, hydrogen bomb, or cobalt bomb [Note 7] is hundreds or even thousands of times [Note 8] the power of the atomic bombs dropped on Hiroshima and Nagasaki in year 1945. When several of the most powerful types of nuclear bombs explode in the stratosphere, human beings become extinct. Nuclear radiation and nuclear dust from nuclear explosions bring "nuclear winter" and nuclear doomsday. [Note 9] Eventually, the glaciers melt away. All land and oceans are flooded with radiation and poisons. Animals and plants die out, all human beings are killed out, and ultimately the destruction of the earth indefinitely.

The Doomsday Clock is a symbol that represents the likelihood of a man-made global catastrophe. It's set up since 1947 by the members of the Bulletin of the Atomic Scientists, the clock is a metaphor for threats to humanity from unchecked scientific and technical advances. Since 2010, the clock has been moved forward over 4 minutes, and has changed by 6 minutes and 20 seconds since 1947. [Note 10] It's the closest time to midnight, the doomsday, only 100 seconds away at the end of year 2020. In January 2021, the clock's setting was left unchanged.

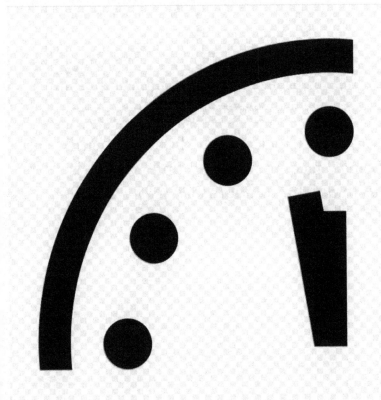

The Doomsday Clock pictured at its current setting of "100 seconds to midnight, the doomsday" in year 2020 and no change now in year 2021 [Note 10]

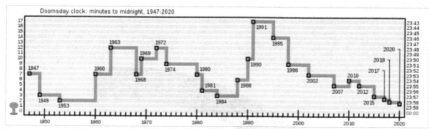
Doomsday Clock graph, 1947–2020. The lower points on the graph represent a higher probability of technologically or environmentally-induced catastrophe, and the higher points represent a lower probability.

The Doomsday Clock graph lists the earth and human beings face the closest time which is "100 seconds to midnight, to doomsday [Note 10]

34

3 THE EARTH FORMING A SINGLE UNITED NATIONS IN ACCORDANCE WITH THE NEW UNITED NATIONS CONSTITUTION

There is still much room for improvement in the evolution of capitalism and communism. It's good that capitalism advocates free development and respects individual free will. However, excessive emphasis on the level of free competition and vertical/horizontal integration of the wealth concentration of TRUST has caused serious inequality between the rich and the poor in the society.

The goal of communism at the beginning was "everyone does what he can and takes what he needs." It was good at the beginning but then went astray, when materialistic thinking was added to eliminate the improvement of the mind and spirit. Communism was even more wrong when Bolshevism with violent methods were covered. After the founding of the country, the Communists setup a constitution that prohibits opposition to the leadership of the Communist Party and the country. According to this, others are not allowed to oppose the leadership of the Communist Party, and others are not allowed to criticize the Communist Party. Therefore, there is room for improvement in political freedom, freedom of speech, freedom of association, freedom of the press, academic freedom, religious freedom, and democracy. Opponents under the Communist government are monitored and intimidated, and even imprisoned with severe sentences for treason. When a party only allows the party to lead the government and country, and does not allow non-party members to join the government, treats all the people as potential enemies, monitors them, and applies severe penalties to deal with the people who oppose it, then the party must reflect on how to accept the suggestions of the people and improve. After all, if a group does not allow all the people to oppose it or suggest, it must have a conscience not to oppose the free will of all the people. Otherwise, it is possible for only one or a very small number of the leaders to make seriously wrong decisions which results in a war. Local wars lead to global nuclear wars, which will eventually destroy the earth and all human beings.

The earth forming a single country, the new
United Nations

Some transparent system and solution of
"Politics and System" is also listed as follows.
Taking the current "United Nations, UN" as
the framework and the European Union (EU)
as a reference, we need to further optimize and
update a new United Nations constitution to
make the earth a single country, that is, the
current name of the "United Nations".
Hereinafter, it is directly referred to as the
"United Nations, UN". Now any country will
only be a state (or province) under the
jurisdiction of the UN. Under the love and
respect of free will, all human beings are born
equal, regardless of skin color, race, gender,
age, religion, language, customs, occupation,
property, region, state (provincial) nationality
or social origin, political opinion or other all
unprohibited opinions are protected by
equality. Everyone enjoys the rights of
democracy, freedom, equality and also personal
and property security, and is protected by all
the Universal Declaration of Human Rights. In

addition, all information is transparent, and there must be no opaque information that can cause corruption. The resolutions of the United Nations Congress are announced daily. All adults in the UN have information products to conduct national politics and national elections. Major UN resolutions and important issues, such as those related to contact with extraterrestrial civilizations, are decided by the UN referendum. New laws enacted by the UN and legal updates must be decided by more than two-thirds of the UN referendum.

When the goal of love and mutual assistance is realized, the world was shared by the public and all people, rather than seeking the private interests of oneself (a party or a group). Politics is based on public opinion, and the system is established in accordance with the United Nations Constitution and various decrees, which is transparent and in line with the interests of the whole people. Choose virtuous people such as those who are with high morals and recommend talented people such as those who have made outstanding contributions to technology or systems to form the UN government. Every state can elect one Congressman of the UN. For the state whose total population exceeds by the different levels of 100 million, 300 million, 1 billion, or 3 billion people, one more Congressman can be elected. For example, if the total population of a state exceeds 300 million, but does not reach 1 billion, the state can elect three Congressmen. All UN Congressmen form the UN Congress, which supervises and corrects the UN government. The United Nations Government Civil Service Organization Law is enacted and passed by the UN referendum. The government serves the people, and must not monitor and oppress the people. The UN Congressmen and UN civil servants are public servants of the people, serving the people as their duty. The government is authorized by the people to serve the people, not to supervise the people, let alone oppress the people. The government is composed of virtuous and talented civil servants and serves the people in transparent and fair systems. Under transparent and fair systems, land, farmland, housing and office buildings and all real estate are owned by self-users, self-employed farmers, or joint-farms instead of being occupied by non-self-users to exploit others. Non-self-users can sell real estate for non-self-use, and invest in other items to avoid driving up and manipulating prices of farmland and real estate, and increasing rents to exploit self-users, self-employed farmers or joint-farms. In this way, the ideals of farmers owning land and residents owning houses are achieved, and the rights of non-self-use people who own farmland, houses/apartments, shops, offices are also taken into consideration.

The UN assists the states in the overall planning of funds, rationally plan and build education systems at all levels and in line with the professional needs and plan for all marriage, birth, medical care and free homes for the elderly. Extensively establish free supplementary education institutions for preschool (zero to six years old) children as well. Provide free compulsory education for students aged six to eighteen. Develop legitimate leisure and entertainment venues, and plan for the supply, demand and development of employment for scholars/researchers, farmers, industry, commerce and various occupations, so that education and employment can match and meet social needs. Widely build free homes for the elderly. Set up institutions and facilities to serve those in need. Showing the spirit of love and mutual assistance, everyone not only loves their own family, but also extends to the loved ones of others. Not only raise their own children, but also help raise the children of others. Employed men and women can have ideal jobs before retirement in twenty-five years of work, can display their talents and improve the world's progress. Both men and women of marriageable age can find suitable partners for marriage then plan childbirth. Provide the elderly with life-long care treatment and institutions. The young people can have the treatment and institutions for nurturing and education to facilitate growth. The old widowers and old widows, the bereaved young orphans, the old and childless elders, and the disabled can be taken care of. The above are transparent systems and solutions for "Politics and Systems" and "Food, Clothing, Housing, Transportation, Education, and entertainment".

Reforms will reduce or lose their interests to those with vested interested and their interest groups, and will surely compensate those who have lost their interests under transparent and fair systems. However, a very small number of improper and exclusive benefit holders and their interest groups in power will vigorously instigate counterattacks. We must persist in good reforms then guide and dissolve the aggressive counterattacks of interest groups with love and mutual assistance. As long as it is reformed into democratic, free, fair and transparent systems to achieve democratic, free and fair society without hunger and cold. Thus, there will be no refugees, no exploitation, no struggles and wars, and there must not and surely no bloody revolution. The reform of the UN makes all systems transparent and legally fair for all human beings, and the reform will surely compensate a small number of those whose interests have suffered and take into account the rights and interests of all human beings.

4 ACHIEVING LOVE AND MUTUAL ASSISTANCE THROUGH LOVE EDUCATION

Education is the most important foundation of human beings. We all receive free compulsory education between the ages of six and eighteen. The education emphasizes love and mutual assistance, improves moral/spiritual level and the well-being and progress of all human beings. Nowadays, education is biased towards utilitarianism and focuses on personal success, but less teaches human morality and spiritual improvement, and the well-being and progress of all human beings. Besides, almost all human beings also emphasize how individuals can win, how to make big money, and emphasize material pursuits. Therefore, the thick black doctrine and wolf thought are correspondingly popular. The social climate to gain money and material creates a trend of unscrupulous means for seeking ends. Video games and online games are full of pornography and violence, and the media is also sensationalizing and exaggerating negative reports, so that people are unscrupulous in seeking to maximize money and fulfill material desires. The governments should improve the contents of education for moral and spiritual improvement and the well-being and progress of all human beings. Video games and online games should eliminate pornography and violence. The media also eliminates grandstanding and negative reports, promotes kindness but suppresses evil, and fulfills its responsibility for social information dissemination. The above is the transparent system and solution for "education".

Free Education with Love and Mutual Assistance for All

Freedom does not affect the freedom of others as its scope. Education must emphasize the importance of individual free will, and the legal individual free must be respected and protected to the utmost. The governments respect the free will of the people, and must not maximize the interests of the UN, the state, or a certain group of parties in order to monitor or intimidate the people and suppress the free will of individuals. Public servants are well aware of the law and master public implements and powers. If they deliberately violate the law in order to hinder the free will of the people, this part aggravates the criminal liability. If anyone's democracy, freedom, equality or any rights are violated, human beings must uphold the spirit of mutual love and mutual assistance, and do their utmost to help him. In the spirit of mutual love and mutual assistance, nobody is treated unfairly.

The level of science and technology has been greatly improved recently, but not only has the spirituality not improved significantly, some items have even regressed. For example, some people add their own deviant thought to a certain religion, and carry out planned and undifferentiated terrorist attacks. Prolonged wars in certain countries due to differences in religious sects or beliefs have resulted in heavy casualties and many refugees. Certain countries suppress opposite opinions and ideas, and use the authority of individual party or minority organization or group to manipulate the country, maximizing the private interests of minority group or party, and infringing on the rights of the people. Powerful countries around the world may be on the brink of war due to conflicts of interest or for their own self-interest, regardless of the safety of the world and human beings. Thus, a small war may cause a nuclear war to destroy the earth and kill all human beings. It can be therefore seen the importance of love and mutual assistance to achieve "the World of Great Harmony" which is to replace hatred, selfishness, violence and nuclear wars so as to prevent the destruction of all human beings and the earth.

5 BASIC FOOD/CLOTHING AND FREE FROM FEAR

In order to avoid exchange rate/financial manipulation, improper interests, money laundering due to crimes and seek for stable economy of the UN, the Quantum World Dollar (World Dollar, WD), issued and managed by the UN, becomes the unified and only currency on the earth within one year of the founding of the new UN, which replaces all other currencies including virtual currencies. The United Nations Financial Center (UNFC), which connects with the states and the UN, is set up to prevent improper manipulation of interests and harm to the economy under the jurisdiction of the UN, and to protect the financial interests of everyone. The UN helps the states to investigate and ban organized crimes such as drug trafficking, smuggling, corruption, money laundering, gambling, fraud, human trafficking, violent intimidation and all crimes and prevent money laundering to help maintain the law and order of the earth and all human beings. With the services of the UN and governments at all levels, human beings have no worries about food and clothing. When anyone's total WD amount in the account at the UNFC connected to the UN and each state is lower than the "Basic Daily Expenditure per Person, BDEP", the system automatically adds his total WD amount to no less than the BDEP amount. The BDEP amount is set up and updated by the UN and helps human beings to satisfy basic need and free from fear, so that crimes due to lack of food, clothing and basic needs can be eliminated. The BDEP amount is used for personal basic food, clothing and other need per day. If it is not used on the same day, it will be automatically invalidated and cannot be added to the second day to become twice of the BDEP amount. Everyone who is employed is entitled to the WD amount, which is automatically booked in the account at the UNFC. Everyone can withdraw limited WD amount per day from the ATM (automated teller machine) or the bank(s) connected to the UNFC. When a large WD amount is withdrawn from an account connected at the UNFC, the purpose must be indicated for future reference, so as to avoid deliberate withdrawal of total WD amount to be less than the BDEP amount for arbitrage. Non-violation of the law and with the "Moral Level Enhancement, MLE" can also increase an individual's WD amount. The WD amount of the "MLE" is also set up and updated by the UN. The above are transparent systems and solutions for "food, clothing, transportation and entertainment".

The legal assets and funds other than the non-self-use premises before the establishment of the new UN should be protected. It is recommended that the whole UN has only one comprehensive income tax system for enterprises and individuals. The individual comprehensive income tax rate for the amount of personal comprehensive income exceeding 26 times the annual minimum wage of individuals in the state shall not be lower than 99%, as shown in the following example. The amount donated to private institutions or private foundations cannot be included as a deduction for the taxable income of individuals or any company. Under the comprehensive social welfare of "the World of Great Harmony", everyone has no shortage of food, clothing, housing, transportation, education, entertainment, medical care and all social welfare.

Multiples of minimum wage / Personal income range	Income tax rate	Personal income range	Income tax	After-tax income	Cummulated after-tax income	Cummulated income	Comprehensive Income tax rate
0	0%	20,000	-	20,000	20,000	20,000	0.00%
2 times ~2.5 times (incl.)	2.00%	5,000	100	4,900	24,900	25,000	0.40%
2.5 times ~3 times (incl.)	6.00%	5,000	300	4,700	29,600	30,000	1.33%
3 times ~4 times (incl.)	8.00%	10,000	800	9,200	38,800	40,000	3.00%
4 times ~5 times (incl.)	10.00%	10,000	1,000	9,000	47,800	50,000	4.40%
5 times ~6 times (incl.)	12.00%	10,000	1,200	8,800	56,600	60,000	5.67%
6 times ~7 times (incl.)	14.00%	10,000	1,400	8,600	65,200	70,000	6.86%
7 times ~8 times (incl.)	16.00%	10,000	1,600	8,400	73,600	80,000	8.00%
8 times ~9 times (incl.)	18.00%	10,000	1,800	8,200	81,800	90,000	9.11%
9 times ~10 times (incl.)	20.00%	10,000	2,000	8,000	89,800	100,000	10.20%
10 times ~11 times (incl.)	25.00%	10,000	2,500	7,500	97,300	110,000	11.55%
11 times ~12 times (incl.)	30.00%	10,000	3,000	7,000	104,300	120,000	13.08%
12 times ~13 times (incl.)	35.00%	10,000	3,500	6,500	110,800	130,000	14.77%
13 times ~14 times (incl.)	40.00%	10,000	4,000	6,000	116,800	140,000	16.57%
14 times ~15 times (incl.)	50.00%	10,000	5,000	5,000	121,800	150,000	18.80%
15 times ~16 times (incl.)	55.00%	10,000	5,500	4,500	126,300	160,000	21.06%
16 times ~17 times (incl.)	60.00%	10,000	6,000	4,000	130,300	170,000	23.35%
17 times ~18 times (incl.)	65.00%	10,000	6,500	3,500	133,800	180,000	25.67%
18 times ~19 times (incl.)	70.00%	10,000	7,000	3,000	136,800	190,000	28.00%
19 times ~20 times (incl.)	75.00%	10,000	7,500	2,500	139,300	200,000	30.35%
20 times ~21 times (incl.)	80.00%	10,000	8,000	2,000	141,300	210,000	32.71%
21 times ~22 times (incl.)	85.00%	10,000	8,500	1,500	142,800	220,000	35.09%
22 times ~23 times (incl.)	90.00%	10,000	9,000	1,000	143,800	230,000	37.48%
23 times ~24 times (incl.)	95.00%	10,000	9,500	500	144,300	240,000	39.88%
24 times ~25 times (incl.)	97.00%	10,000	9,700	300	144,600	250,000	42.16%
25 times ~26 times (incl.)	98.00%	10,000	9,800	200	144,800	260,000	44.31%
26 times ~27 times (incl.)	99.00%	10,000	9,900	100	144,900	270,000	46.33%
27 times ~28 times (incl.)	99.50%	10,000	9,950	50	144,950	280,000	48.23%
28 times ~30 times (incl.)	99.70%	20,000	19,940	60	145,010	300,000	51.66%
30 times ~40 times (incl.)	99.90%	100,000	99,900	100	145,110	400,000	63.72%
40 times ~60 times (incl.)	99.92%	200,000	199,840	160	145,270	600,000	75.79%
60 times ~80 times (incl.)	99.94%	200,000	199,880	120	145,390	800,000	81.83%
80 times ~100 times (incl.)	99.96%	200,000	199,920	80	145,470	1,000,000	85.45%
100 times ~120 times (incl.)	99.98%	200,000	199,960	40	145,510	1,200,000	87.87%
120 times ~140 times (incl.)	99.99%	200,000	199,980	20	145,530	1,400,000	89.61%
140 times ~160 times (incl.)	99.99%	200,000	199,980	20	145,550	1,600,000	90.90%
160 times ~	99.99%						

Recommended comprehensive income tax rate example for individuals

Transfer personal funds to new personal accounts when "the World of Great Harmony" is set up?	One comprehensive personal income tax rate when "the World of Great Harmony" is set up?
Yes. Personal funds will be totally transferred to the new personal accounts	Yes. Per new rate due to no tremendous fund needed under the society with complete social welfare

New comprehensive income tax rate due to no tremendous fund needed under the society with complete social welfare

The existing funds before "the World of Great Harmony" remain unchanged. With comprehensive care under "the World of Great Harmony", it is unnecessary for individuals, private non-profit organizations or private foundations to increase a huge amount of additional assets hereafter. The high taxes of the high-income earners help "the World of Great Harmony" achieve perfect social welfare, which is a manifestation of love and mutual assistance. The higher progressive tax rate is for the UN and all levels of governments to provide social welfare and services for all. Those who deliberately evade tax will be fined from five to ten times the amount of tax evasion. The maximum personal comprehensive income tax rate cannot be lower than 99.99%. Everyone's personal monthly minimum salary/wage must not be less than 30% of the state's average income.

The UN assists the states in setting up more medical and nursing departments in schools, so that there will be a large number of doctors and nurses for medical system. The research and development of medicine is mainly to help people with low-price healthcare, but does not aim at profit generating or for accumulating personal wealth. In accordance with the spirit of Taiwan's sound and affordable National Health Insurance (NHI), the fair NHI system is widely implemented in all states. It is supplemented by AI (artificial intelligence) to assist medical staff to reduce manpower. All people afford low-price NHI premium and a low percentage of medical deductibles, so that they will not go bankrupt due to high medical expenses. When one UN citizen's WD amount is too low to pay the NHI premium or medical expense deductible, the entire difference is divided by half of the UN and the state. The above are related to some transparent systems and solutions for "taxation, education and medical/healthcare".

"Residents have their own houses" is a human ideal

"Residents have their own houses" is a human ideal. Houses/apartments, shops, offices and land are for human use, not for exploitation. **"Don't do to others what you don't want to do to yourself."** It's not fair that anyone wants to his own house but can't afford it, or bears high mortgage and interest expenses to make him and/or his family impoverished and almost breathless. Since we don't want to be so painful, we should put ourselves in the thinking that we must not become the pain-makers to make countless people who need houses/apartments at metropolitan area but cannot afford them. The high housing price in the metropolitan area is the real pain point while an uninhabited ancestral house or a holiday house in the suburbs 50 kilometers away from downtown is not included in the calculation of residential housing in the metropolitan area because it does not cause pain to others. It is unreasonable to pay high rents to landlords from those who do not own houses/apartments, shops, offices and land. In particular, unsound laws and tax rates allow landlords to own many houses/apartments, shops, offices and land for huge profits from lessee. At present, the price of real estate is even extremely higher. The UN and the states establish reasonable land and housing regulations, tax systems, and rent caps to enable users to have their own houses/apartments, shops, offices. The yearly real estate tax rate of self-use houses/apartments, shops and offices is even with 10% discount at the current tax rate. The real estate tax of the first set of non-self-use houses/apartments, shops, offices in the metropolitan area is 80% or 90% of the current average annual rent in the market. The real estate tax of the second set of non-self-use houses/apartments, shops, offices in the metropolitan area is a multiple (e.g. double) of the current average annual rent in the market. The real estate tax of the third set or above of non-self-use houses/apartments, shops, offices in the metropolitan area is even a much higher multiple (e.g. triple) of the current average annual rent in the market. Regardless of whether it is rented or not, the real estate tax in the metropolitan area is not tax deductible.

The tax rate of non-self-use real estate in the metropolitan area will be adjusted gradually, and it is recommended that the tax rate adjustment target be reached in five years. The above adjustments will gradually reduce the prices of real estate and land then reach reasonable prices. The gradual adjustment of the tax rate for non-self-use premises in the metropolitan area will enable multiple sets of non-self-use premises in the metropolitan area to be sold at a still not low price in exchange for cash in the first several years. The state government sets a high percentage of real estate transaction income tax rate (for example 95%) to the seller's total transaction benefits to avoid huge profits from hoarding real estate but enhance public interest. In this way, the seller has reasonable but minor benefits and obtains cash, the buyer has reasonable acquisition costs, the government has high taxes on transaction benefits, and imposes higher tax rates and tax amounts on those who insist on hoarding houses/apartments, shops, offices and land for profiteering. This achieves the purpose of the public owning the profit of sale of real estate and the effect of stabilizing housing and land prices. Taking into account the rights and interests of real estate owners, the government has high taxes to serve all people to enhance public welfare, and achieve a win-win situation of the human ideal of "Residents have their own houses". In this way, the seller is required to pay a high percentage (for example, 95%) tax rate of the total transaction benefit. Therefore, hoarding houses/apartments, shops, offices and land not only cannot make huge profits, but the high tax rate of non-self-use real estate in the metropolitan area is also not conducive to the long-term holding of many houses/apartments, shops, offices and/or land hoarders for profit. If real estate prices fall, it will even cause losses. Under such a perfect system, organized and individuals are not willing to hoard houses/apartments, shops, offices and land, but gradually sell them, and transfer the funds to other more meaningful investments. The prices of houses/departments, shops and offices in metropolitan areas will become more reasonable. Those who want to buy their own houses/departments, shops and offices in the metropolitan area will be able to purchase them at a relatively reasonable price, then the human ideal of "Residents have their own houses" can be easily and perfectly achieved. The above is a transparent system and solution for "housing".

6 UN SOLDIERS AND WEAPONS NOT TO DEAL WITH HUMAN BEINGS UNLESS ARMED INSURGENT GROUPS

The followings are some transparent systems and solutions for "politics/systems and contact with extraterrestrial civilizations". The military is only affiliated to the UN, not to any state. It only protects the earth and human beings, explores extraterrestrials beyond the earth, communicates with extraterrestrial civilizations, deals with the intrusion of extraterrestrial civilizations (should be none) if any, and prevents meteorites or star impacts. Nuclear bombs and destructive weapons belong only to the UN military. The use of UN soldiers and weapons is subject to the approval of the UN Congress. Unless more than three-quarters of the UN Congress passes a resolution to resolve armed rebellions or collective criminal groups, UN soldiers and weapons shall not deal with human beings.

UN soldiers and weapons shall not deal with human beings (Refer to photo at http://www.51yuansu.com/sc/ssrnjgggwg.html)

In the UN, state security agencies are responsible for state security and border control. The UN assists the police in the states to detect and prohibit organized crimes such as drug trafficking, smuggling, corruption, money laundering, gambling, fraud, human trafficking, kidnapping, violent intimidation and all other crimes, in order to maintain the law and order of the earth and all human beings. The state borders may not fully open for the time being due to many differences among the states upon the establishment of the UN. Border opening can be implemented in different states, and there is no need to be totally consistent in the UN. The individual and full opening of the border are passed and implemented by more than three-quarters of the UN Congress. If more than three-quarters of the UN Congress passes a certain state to implement border opening, while the citizens of the state veto the border opening by more than three-quarters of the vote within one month of the UN resolution, the state resolution must still be respected and followed. Only a year later can the UN continue to mention the state's implementation of border opening.

The era of information asymmetry is over. They (the summits of the great powers) cannot continue to use the policy of fooling the people to cover up the facts of extraterrestrial civilizations. Under the coordination of the UN, knowledge of the universe and extraterrestrial civilizations will be immediately made public. There are countless extraterrestrial civilizations in the universe, and almost all extraterrestrial civilizations are peace-loving. Their technology is so superb that they can unhide their appearance and vessels when they want us to see them, but hide them when they don't want us to see them. Besides, they can apply transformation technology of universe dimension that we can't imagine, and reach the earth extremely quickly. If they want to attack the earth per their advanced technology and ability, it is not difficult. We don't have to be afraid of the coming contact with extraterrestrial civilizations, and fear is useless. The comers must be good and friendly. If extraterrestrial civilizations were not friendly and would invade the earth, our ancestors would have perished thousands of years before. Since the technology and ability of extraterrestrial civilizations far surpasses us, we do not take the initiative to contact them. If they would like to directly communicate and help us. We communicate with them through the only window, the UN. We don't need to be afraid. It's great to have friends coming from afar!

7 SHARING RESOURCES AND COOPERATION WITH EACH OTHER

At present, energy is mainly based on burning fossil fuels to generate electricity. Fossil fuels include coal, oil and natural gas. Burning fossil fuels produces a large amount of carbon dioxide, which further worsens the impact of global warming of the earth. Although the utilization of hydrogen energy and various renewable energy sources continues to increase slightly, they still cannot replace fossil fuel energy. Concentrated solar power (CSP) [Note 11] system is a power generation system by applying lenses or mirrors to concentrate a large area of sunlight onto a receiver then transform to power. Concentrated photovoltaics (CPV) [Note 11] system is another technology to generate power by sunlight. The solar CPV / CSP hybrid system can be more efficient than traditional solar power systems. It is recommended to increase/adjust the heliostat fields and the solar power towers to improve power generation efficiency. In addition, the use of convex lenses to focus and convert sunlight into heat and then into electricity is another clean energy source. Although only sunlight can generate power during the day, when there is sunlight to generate energy during the day, it is in line with the peak electricity consumption. And this facility which is a high-efficiency clean energy with only around 5% of the ground needed compared with the general solar power systems. The hybrid system of solar CPV / CSP system and lens focusing sunlight into energy greatly improves the energy efficiency. And quantum fission and fusion to generate power is another effective, safe and clean energy.

"Future energy" is much powerful, and if used maliciously, it will cause devastating disasters, so human beings are still unable to obtain it. When the morality and spirituality of all human beings are raised to a certain level and when the powerful energy will not be used for military violence and harm to living beings, human beings will obtain "future energy". At that time, "future energy" will replace fossil fuel energy and become mainstream energy sources, which improves carbon dioxide emissions and the impact of global warming of the earth. When human beings obtain "future energy", the UN will set up "future energy" plants in various places to avoid waste of energy due to long-distance energy transmission.

Human Beings loving and cooperating from now on

The breakthrough point of traffic and movement is to overcome the gravity of the earth. Before we can get more advanced technology, we can fly with ultrasonic levitation to overcome the gravity of the earth and apply the automatic transmission and reflection of ultrasonic waves to fly safely. The above is another transparent system and solution for "transportation". Human beings in three-dimensional space cannot ascend to a higher dimension because the moral level is not high enough to obtain more advanced technology that transforms dimensional/space-time. Otherwise, those who are with low moral may apply dimensional/space-time transformation technology to return to the past to enable themselves or their immediate elders to buy lottery to win billion dollars; or to harm opponents or enemies. Such misuse will confuse time and space. And even abuse by extremely selfish people will cause the consequences of destruction. Therefore, if human beings cannot improve the current moral and spiritual level, not only will we not be able to obtain higher technology and ability of dimensional/space-time transformation, but now nuclear wars resulted from selfish and hatred can destroy all human beings and the earth.

The same type of industry and upstream/downstream industries should be located in the same industrial zone as far as possible to reduce transportation costs and reduce waste. Integrate the mutual support and use of resources and energy in the industrial zone, and exchange the use of energy, resources and various projects to improve the overall efficiency and synergy of the use of energy and resources. Comprehensive consideration and utilization of various industrial gases or other resources produced by cogeneration systems, waste heat recovery or other methods, as well as oxygen, hydrogen, etc., and exchange excess energy and resources with neighboring industrial areas to achieve a combination of energy and resources integration and synergy. The waste and scrap are "recycled and reused", and water and other resources are recycled as well. Idle industrial land and factory buildings shall not be hoarded for profit. The state governments announce the suggested prices of land and factory buildings in each industrial zone, and coordinate the transaction between buyers and sellers to achieve a win-win situation. The state governments set up a high percentage (for example 95%) of the seller's total transaction benefits as the tax rate, which achieves the purpose of the public owning the profit of sale of real estate in industrial areas. In this way, the sellers have reasonable but minor profit on sale of the real estate, the buyers have a reasonable cost of acquiring the land and plants in the industrial zones, and the governments have a high percentage of the transaction benefit as tax, which achieves win-win situation. Meanwhile, the purposes of the public owning the profit of sale of real estate and stabilizing the price of the land and plants in the industrial areas. The earth's energy and various resources are shared by all human beings, not for private or exclusive use by a state, and the goal of making the best use of everything is achieved. The UN must compensate for the pollution caused by resource mining and development, and if there is damage to the environment or protection issues, it must be remedied. The above are some transparent systems and solutions for "housing, employment and industry".

8 ENVIRONMENTAL PROTECTION AND LOVE FOR THE EARTH

The following is transparent system and solution for "environmental protection". The earth is the mother of all human beings and nourishes us so that we should well treat and protect the earth. In addition to protecting the earth, the mountains, waters, soils, rocks, minerals, plants, and animals on the earth all have their spirituality. We should also treat and protect them. If we need to use them, we must be grateful and use them in accordance with the law. If there is a massive decline or endangerment of species, or the environmental protection of the place is damaged, it must be remedied. At the same time, we need to try to supplement various resources for sustainable operation.

The mountains, waters, soils, rocks, minerals, plants, and animals on the earth all have their spirituality

The UN is committed to developing clean energy, avoiding pollution, advocating the recycling, reusing materials, reducing the generation and discharge of garbage and pollutants, and trying to clean pollutants that have been discharged on land, underground, air and sea. Pay attention to the principles of economical use, repeated application and recycling, and do not waste resources and food. Buy unpackaged or less packaged goods, choose goods made from recycled paper pulp or materials, buy second-hand goods or go to the second-hand exchange market for environmentally friendly items. Garbage disposal is based on the principles of "garbage classification", "resource recycling", and "reuse". Shorten the mileage of commodities and food, try to purchase local and seasonal agricultural products, buy local commodities, and reduce the purchase of imported or remotely transported commodities, so as to reduce the cost and energy of refrigeration, insulation, transportation and storage. As for recreation, transportation and travel need to be greener, more leisurely, and more localized. The COVID-19 pandemic has changed the tourism and aviation industries, and more leisure and environmentally friendly means of transportation such as walking and bicycles have been favored, and cities have added dedicated bicycle lanes. Air travelers prefer to travel within countries (states) and short-term trip, so that everyone can discover the beauty of their cities and places. Tourists also try their best to choose to experience locally. Pay attention to environmental protection when traveling, choose a green hotel, bring environmental protection appliances, light luggage, and participate in environmental protection and green itineraries. Use various technologies to achieve the goals of energy saving, environmental protection, carbon reduction and pollution reduction. We need to be committed to environmental protection of food, environmental protection of clothing, environmental protection of home and work place, environmental protection of transportation, environmental protection of living habits, and environmental protection of all human beings.

Environmental protection is the responsibility of all human beings

When all human beings pay attention on environmental protection anywhere and anytime, it is the day to treat and protect the earth. Mother Earth selflessly nourishes human beings and all things, how can we not protect Mother Earth?

9 GREENHOUSE CROPS AND OPTIMIZED FOOD

Since we have neglected environmental protection in the past and harmed the earth's environment, now we bear the counterattack of nature caused by harming the earth's environment. The earth's environment is changing day by day. Nowadays, there are often persistent droughts, fires, heavy rains, hurricanes, abnormally high or low temperatures, causing crop shortage. The more critical issue is that the impact of global warming causes the higher sea level. Besides, the more frequent volcanoes, earthquakes, tsunamis and future geomagnetic deflection or stellar collisions will even endanger the survival of human beings. Since we harm the earth's environment, we are now incurring various disasters. In the future, only when human beings abandon selfishness, but loves and help each other, make up for and recover the damage to the earth's environment, can the impact of disasters be reduced. The UN assists states in optimizing food and crop breeding, and planting optimized food and crops with high production efficiency in the regions based on topography, rainfall, temperature and various factors around the world. Build large-scale of high-volume and high-productivity solar greenhouses in various places to stably cultivate greenhouse food, fruits, vegetables and crops. Develop artificial food, such as artificial protein, to cope with food shortage, transportation concern and storage problems caused by weather changes, and to provide a stable and continuous supply per human needs.

The UN assists states in optimizing food and crops breeding

The UN works with the states to automatically produce various products in appropriate areas to stabilize human needs for food, clothing, housing, transportation, education, and entertainment. Not only solve the employment problem, but also improve the consequences of insufficient problem and/or overproduction. The UN assists states in establishing climate-smart agricultural technology to enhance agricultural and industrial resilience. Maintain and upgrade the production environment and resources, build a disaster warning and response system, and reduce climate risks and damage. Strengthen disaster relief and insurance systems, and improve agricultural and industrial risk management and response capabilities. The UN assists states in storing dry, sterile, and sealed food to cope with food shortages caused by sudden annual or consecutive years of climate change. When a state is short of food, the UN assists in distribution among states and the states help each other. human beings work together, love and help each other. The above are some other transparent systems and solutions for " Food, clothing, housing, transportation, education and entertainment".

10 HUMAN BEINGS LOVING EACH OTHER AND "THE WORLD OF GREAT HARMONY"

The reason for applying "the World of Great Harmony" instead of "The Republic" or "Utopia" is because the "the World of Great Harmony" has sound systems and is indeed feasible, rather than an empty ideal, and there are no classes and no mercenaries. The political system of "the World of Great Harmony" is a system for the whole people and a representative system. General issues are voted by the Congress, while important issues are voted by the people. And the principle of distinguishing between general and important issues is determined by a referendum. It is not difficult to achieve "the World of Great Harmony", but it's as simple as a single decision and persistence of ours. When the whole earth is built as a single country based on the above-mentioned transparent systems and solutions, it is the new UN. Under the sound systems, we select candidates who agree to love/mutual assistance and "the World of Great Harmony". Then "the World of Great Harmony" can be gradually achieved in accordance with procedures and steps planned by the congress. For the countries/regions that are still undemocratic, we can appeal the needs of love/mutual assistance and "the World of Great Harmony" through demonstrations and rational/legal means until the ideal is realized, but refrain from resorting to violence and crimes. The army, the police and all public security organs must stand with the people and justice, refrain from protecting the dictator(s) to become the enemy of the people and justice. We work together to abandon hatred, struggle, wars leading a nuclear war, but embrace love/mutual assistance, peace and happiness of "the World of Great Harmony"!

Animals are based on the principle of competition, while human beings are based on the principle of mutual assistance. Animals fight for food or the pursuit of the opposite sex. Nowadays, some human beings also do everything they can to fight for property or seek interest of theirs (or a party or a country). Individual or collective crimes can be sanctioned by law, while wars cause serious casualties and severe damage to human beings, species and the earth. Powerful countries' wars even cause nuclear wars which destroy human beings and the earth. Under the crisis of destroying human beings and the earth, how can we protect ourselves? How can we take the responsibility of protecting the earth and all species? Only when we, human beings, elevate our moral level and spirituality, return to love and mutual assistance, can we enter the ideal state of everyone: "the World of Great Harmony". We are different from animals because we have ideals, love and help each other, be compassionate, and understand the importance of improving morality and spirituality. If we only know to fight for the needs, and even fight to the death and to the end, by unscrupulous means, how is this different from animals? If it causes wars, or even leads to a nuclear war, which destroys all human beings and the earth, is this the intention of the leaders of powerful countries? The reform of raising the moral level and spirituality to return to love and mutual assistance builds a world of democracy, freedom and prosperity with transparent and fair systems, which benefits everyone.

The reforms will reduce or lose the interests of a small number of people who have vested interests and their interest groups, and the reform will surely compensate those who have lost their interests. A very small number of people with improper power and exclusive interests and their interest groups will fight back vigorously. However, we must persist when there is any vigorous counterattack and guide and influence them with love

and mutual assistance. **As long as it is reformed into a democratic, free, fair and transparent systems to achieve a democrat, free, fair and just UN, there will be no refugees, no exploitation, no struggles and wars, and there must not be any bloody revolution. This is an important process of transforming from selfishness, hatred, struggle, war and destruction to love, mutual assistance, harmony, peace and happiness.** In this process, everyone is the beneficiary. Meanwhile, the wisdom and foresight of the leaders of major powers and Freemasonry and Illuminati are very critical in this process. The whole world and society must respect the free will of individuals, at least the free will of the majority of people. When everyone's brainstorming and the final decision of love and mutual assistance is accepted and practiced, "the World of Great Harmony" will not be far away.

Since we don't want to live in undemocratic, unfree country or society with expensive medical fee, exhausted work but heavy debts, low social welfare, poverty or even live in a fearful country that oppresses people, the government, public representatives of all levels, and all of us must take responsibility to change it. The reformed countries become the ones with democracy, freedom, peace, prosperity that respect the people's free will and save the people from fear. We also need to peacefully and democratically express our needs, and elect the leaders and public representatives to reform the new UN into "the World of Great Harmony" with love and mutual assistance rather than vote people who are committed to selfishness. If not, it will not only fail to improve the current situation, but even worsen the status quo.

We have only one earth on which we live. We know the importance of improving morality and spirituality now. With the services of the UN and governments at all levels, we have no worries about food and clothing, love and help each other. When some persons have difficulties, others help each other. When some states are in trouble, other states help each other. Only in this way can we move towards a happy and harmonious society. Then, all countries on the earth are united into a unified nation, the UN, which is full of love and mutual assistance. We all live together in a happy world with love and mutual assistance. When our collective consciousness is love, the earth becomes "the World of Great Harmony".

"The World of Great Harmony" with love and mutual assistance is a feasible and necessary direction for us. It is possible to start from "the Area of Great Harmony" from an area, such as Taiwan. Why is Taiwan suitable for piloting "the Area of Great Harmony"? Similar to major countries in the world, housing prices in major metropolitan areas in Taiwan are too high, and they are getting higher. The housing price-to-income ratio in Taipei is 15.54 times in the first quarter of year 2021, which means that it takes 15.54 years for Taipei citizens to buy a house/apartment without any other spending. The young generally cannot afford their own houses/apartments, shops and/or offices. It can be seen that the implementation of "the World of Great Harmony" is so important to everyone. In "the World of Great Harmony", the tax system and law on real estate is transparent and fair that all people have their own houses/apartments. The buildings in Taiwan are not beautiful. However, the above two factors do not prevent Taiwan from piloting "the Area of Great Harmony". The following are the advantages of Taiwan being suitable for piloting "the Area of Great Harmony": "democracy, freedom and sound legal system", "convenient and advanced transportation", "good healthcare, excellent and low-priced National Health Insurance", "financial stability and extremely high foreign exchange for civic wealth", "economic prosperity and stability", "high technology and continual improvements", "developed industries", "universal education, especially higher education", "the Chinese culture of four dimensions and eight virtues is deeply rooted in Taiwanese", "almost no problem of discrimination in Taiwan", "Taiwanese are enthusiastic and tolerant of foreign (other state) people and foreign cultures", "good public security and extremely low violent crimes", "good environmental protection concept and execution", "good services from public servants and almost no corruption", "ecologically rich and diversity", "moderate weather, annual average temperature in Taipei is 23.6 degrees Celsius" and "Taiwanese are generally with love" with instances listed below. Excluding manpower support and relief materials, Taiwan donated nearly three hundred million US dollars to Mainland China for the 2008 Wenchuan earthquake in Mainland China, which is much more than any other country and region outside of China/Hong Kong. In addition, excluding manpower support and relief materials, Taiwan also donated more than two hundred million US dollars to Japan for the 311 Great East Japan Earthquake in year 2011, and the amount of Taiwan donation exceeds the total amount of the other ninety-three countries that have donated... etc.

In addition, the United States, Mainland China/Hong Kong/Macao, Canada, Japan, South Korea, North Korea,

Singapore, India, Pakistan, Bangladesh, Sri Lanka, Nepal, Bhutan, Indonesia, Malaysia, Singapore, Brunei, Thailand, Myanmar, Vietnam, Khmer, Laos, Philippines, Kazakhstan, Turkmenistan, Kyrgyz, Uzbekistan, Tajikistan, Georgia, Armenia, Azerbaijan, Saudi Arabia, United Arab Emirates, Qatar, Kuwait, Turkey, Israel, Lebanon, Egypt, Tunisia, Algeria, Morocco, Ethiopia, Somalia, Eritrea, Djibouti, Sudan, South Sudan, Kenya, Nigeria, Uganda, Luanda, Burundi, Tanzania, Democratic Republic of Congo, Central Africa, Congo, Angola, Cameroon, Ghana, Equatorial Guinea, Benin, Togo, Ivory Coast, Senegal, Guinea, Guinea Bissau, Gambia, Sierra Leone, Liberia, Mali, Burkina Faso, Niger, Chad, Mauritania, Gabon, Zambia, Mozambique, Zimbabwe, Namibia, Botswana, Lesotho, Kingdom of Eswatini, Madagascar ,South Africa, Australia, New Zealand, Papua New Guinea, East Timor, Fiji, Micronesia, Nauru, Samoa, Tonga, Vanuatu, Marshall Islands, Palau, Solomon Islands, Kiribati, Tuvalu, Mexico, Cuba, Argentina, Brazil,

Chile, Colombia, Venezuela, Peru, Paraguay, Uruguay, Bolivia, Ecuador, Jamaica, Dominican Republic, Belize, Guatemala, El Salvador, Honduras, Nicaragua, Costa Rica, Panama, Guyana, Suriname, Russia, the European Union, other non-EU countries in Europe and some other countries in Asia, Latin America, Africa and Oceania not mentioned above are also suitable to try out the "the Area of Great Harmony" so that the world can become the "the World of Great Harmony" as soon as possible. It is recommended that all countries in the world gradually reform into the above-mentioned transparent systems and solutions under the current UN structure to establish a new UN, and finally the earth becomes "the World of Great Harmony" with love, mutual assistance and happiness. The ideal of "the World of Great Harmony" was generated in China several thousand years before. Since it's a treasure of China and the world, it's very suitable and very good for Taiwan and Mainland China/Hong Kong/Macao to pilot the "the Area of Great Harmony" in each area under the Greater China Area first. Therefore, the experience in Greater China Area can expand to worldwide to help the earth become "the World of Great Harmony" quickly. In fact, Mainland China is the closest to "the World of Great Harmony", but it may also be the farthest. The land of Mainland China is currently completely owned by the country so that Mainland China can easily solve the sensitive issues of land. The more advanced infrastructure is also another major advantage for Mainland China to become "the Area of Great Harmony". There mustn't be any bloody revolution or war. The one-party dictatorship gradually accepts a totally democratic and free system, then it is easy for the forward-looking leaders to gradually accept the necessary direction of "the World of Great Harmony" that human beings must achieve, and gradually lead the Mainland China to reform into "the Area of Great Harmony" with great foresight and courage. If so, how fortunate the Communist Party of China is! How fortunate China and all human beings are! Otherwise, the persistence of the anti-democracy and anti-freedom by the one-party dictatorship will be a serious stumbling block for "the World of Great Harmony". If a war is caused by the China-India territorial dispute crisis, the Diaoyutai Islands (or Diaoyu Islands or Senkaku Islands) territorial dispute crisis, the South China Sea crisis, or the Taiwan Strait crisis, it will turn into a nuclear war which will destroy the earth and all human beings. A very critical factor of the happiness or demise of human beings depends on whether the leaders of Mainland China and the Communist Party of China are far-sighted or not.

Since Taiwan is so suitable for piloting "the Area of Great Harmony", other countries (states) or areas need to support and should not provoke disputes or conflicts. When the collective consciousness of human beings in this area, Taiwan, is love, everyone has food and clothing, live and work in peace, friendship, mutual assistance, no hatred, no war, no fear. The status of this area is the predecessor of "the World of Great Harmony" to the UN. As a result, "the Area of the Great Harmony" gradually expands to all of the UN. When the collective consciousness of the all human beings is love, the earth becomes "the World of Great Harmony".

Some people, even if they don't believe in the Creator, know that they have a higher self and an ego. The higher self is love and mutual assistance. Under the spirit of our higher self, we are all full of love and mutual assistance, and perform our duties, achieve goals and live happily under all transparent and fair systems. There is no hunger and cold, no refugees, no persecution, full of love and mutual assistance, helping the weak, improving moral level, and further pursuit of spiritual growth. Then the whole earth forms a single country, UN, full of love and mutual assistance, and becomes "the World of Great Harmony". And a very small number of selfish people think that love and mutual assistance are the performance of the weak. They just want to find loopholes, look for what they call the blue ocean, and step on others to be stronger than everyone, richer or more powerful than everyone. However, under transparent and fair systems, all law, tax and information are extremely transparent, the systems help and support all people including the weak, and everyone lives and works in peace and happiness. Extremely selfish people are whimsical, and they only think that they can unwittingly and unscrupulously obtain undistributed wealth, but eventually go to jail for breaking the law. The ego is selfishness, hatred, fear, poverty, struggle, and even the use of force. The further selfishness evolves into war, and the final result of a nuclear war will destroy the earth and all human beings. In recent years, a series of natural disasters and epidemic infectious diseases including the COVID-19 virus and a series of variant viruses are just small warnings to human beings. In the future, larger natural disasters and deadly epidemic infectious diseases will follow. If we still don't love and help each other, the intensive natural disasters, deadly epidemic diseases and wars caused by selfish hatred then a further nuclear war will completely destroy the earth and all human beings. Chinese Mencius quoted a sentence: "Heaven's disasters can be avoided, but one's own iniquity can't be lived." Nowadays, information is popularized, and almost all information is transparent except information of extraterrestrial civilizations. Unlike a few decades ago, when information was not widely available, the manipulator(s) wanted to cover up any real information, just made up a set of excuses and used official statements to prevaricate the past with manipulative media propaganda. Even more unlike hundreds or thousands of years ago, when dogma and Divine Right Kingship thoughts were restrained, education and information were not popularized, so that the people's wisdom was not high, and the ideas of democracy and freedom were not developed. As long as we love and help each other now, we will increase the low vibration frequency from hatred, selfishness, struggle and war to the higher vibration frequency of love, mutual assistance, harmony and peace. Coupled with environmental protection, we love the earth, make up for the damage to the earth, and are grateful to the earth and beings, when the global environment improves and the impact of global warming gets better, the major natural disasters will become smaller and reduced. With love and mutual assistance, human beings abandon hatred, selfishness, fear, war and misery, then build "the World of Great Harmony" with love and mutual assistance. The Chinese proverb says that you can cross a river in the same boat with those who have cultivated with you for a hundred generations, and you can cultivate for a thousand generations to marry your spouse. The current life is about eighty years, so why do we fight for little advantage to cause injury or death? Why can't we love and help each other to improve everyone's happiness? Is it our goal to come to the earth to kill our so-called opponents who are actually our brothers and sisters on the earth, meanwhile we wound ourselves all over the body? Why can't brothers and sisters on the earth love and help each other, then live happily? Is our purpose to cause war, then further cause a nuclear war to destroy the earth and all human beings at all costs? When the whole human beings are full of the belief in mutual love and mutual assistance, after the establishment of the new UN and the establishment of transparent and sound organizations and systems, there will be no hunger, no crime, no fear and no war. When one person is in difficulties, others help each other. When one state is in trouble, other states help each other.

All people are happy under love and mutual assistance, and all are sages under "the World of Great Harmony". If so, even if the earth is not heaven, it is moving towards the goal of heaven! Beloved brothers and sisters, don't you have the slightest touch in your heart to understand the above-mentioned "the World of Great Harmony" with love and mutual assistance that is feasible and must be achieved? Would you still refuse love and mutual assistance but agree with their selfishness and even deliberately insisting on provoking a war, leading to a nuclear war then destroying the earth and all human beings?

"The World of Great Harmony" is not a slogan, but a perfect state for all human beings with plans, procedures, systems and compensation mechanisms. It is not difficult to achieve "the World of Great Harmony", but it is simple per our one decision and persistence. After reading and thinking about this article, you must feel that it's too late to get this content. We are all brothers and sisters on the earth. Let's work together to abandon the destruction of the earth and all human beings due to selfishness, hatred, fear, wars and a further nuclear war, and achieve "the World of Great Harmony" with love, mutual assistance, peace and happiness!

All spirituality with love, mutual assistance, peace and happiness to achieve "the world of Great Harmony"

We, human beings, are rational because we have ideals, and we are great because we practice ideals. Beloved brothers and sisters! We have stood at the turning point of human beings. How can we not see it? The history of human beings has been a series of wars. Nowadays, tens of thousands of nuclear weapons are enough to destroy all human beings and all creatures on the earth. Selfishness, hatred, struggle and wars leads nuclear wars to destroy the earth and all human beings, while love, mutual assistance, peace and happiness helps achieve the great ideal of "the World of Great Harmony". At the turning point of human beings, I choose love, mutual assistance and "the World of Great Harmony". Which would you choose?

I have another dream that must and will come true. This dream is different from Dr. Martin Luther King, Jr.'s and is that we, human beings, love and help each other, then the earth becomes "the World of Great Harmony".

*NOTE:

[1] The Creator mentioned in the book is the God of Judaism/Catholicism/Christianity or Allah of Islam

[2] The concept of "the World of Great Harmony"(Chinese: 大同世界) comes from the chapter of Great Harmony of China's "Book of Rites Luck"(Chinese: 《禮記·禮運》大同章) and the content is as follows.

When the target of love and mutual assistance is realized, the world is shared by the public and all people. Choose virtuous people and recommend talented people. Honest to people, harmony with neighbors and communities. Showing the spirit of mutual love and mutual assistance, everyone not only loves their own family, but also extends to the loved ones of others. Not only raise their own children, but also help raise the children of others. The system allows the elderly to have life-long care treatment and institutions, the workers have proper jogs to display their talents, and the young people can have the treatment and institutions for nurturing and education to facilitate growth. The old widowers and old widows, the bereaved young orphans, the old and childless elders, and the disabled can be taken care of. Both men and women of marriageable age can find suitable partners. The world and resources are shared by the public and all people. The systems are fair and transparent. Everyone is free from fear, has free will and their own share of basic food and clothing, and the related. People will not take property and anything that does not belong to them but only own the share they have. People have everything to do and they perform their duties for both their needs and the public interest. All people are full of love, help each other, have adequate food and clothing, and have completely improved their moral level and spirituality. So, the idea of evil will not arise, and there is no crime. Therefore, we don't need to lock our doors when we go out. This is the "the World of Great Harmony".

[3] Refer to the content about Both Isaac Newton's and Albert Einstein's great contributions to scientific research and their thought about the final answers to questions about the universe from a masterpiece of the God at https://kknews.cc/zh-tw/science/va9j54l.html

[4] Refer to the related content at https://nexusnewsfeed.com/article/conscious ness/what-the-432-hz-miracle-tone-sounds-like-listen-a-healing-frequency-to-raise-your-vibration/

[5] Refer to the diagram at https://www.voltlin.com/blogs/voltlin/the-significance-of-108-why-is-it-so-important

[6] Refer to the related content of the ten most deadly wars in the world at https://kknews.cc/zh-tw/history/xmbxm4q.html and http://www.ifuun.com/a20172151154470/

[7] Refer to some information of cobalt bomb at cobalt bomb content under Wikipedia at https://en.wikipedia.org/wiki/Cobalt_bomb

[8] Refer to some information at https://en.wikipedia.org/wiki/Tsar_Bomba

[9] Refer to some information of nuclear wars at nuclear warfare content under Wikipedia at https://en.wikipedia.org/wiki/Nuclear_warfare

[10] Refer to the Doomsday Clock picture, Doomsday Clock graph and the major content of its current setting of "100 seconds to midnight in year 2020 and now in year 2021 under Wikipedia at https://en.wikipedia.org/wiki/Doomsday_Clock Doomsday Clock - Wikipedia

[11] Refer to the information of Concentrated Solar Power and Concentrator Photovoltaics under Wikipedia at https://en.wikipedia.org/wiki/Concentrated_solar_power and

https://en.wikipedia.org/wiki/Concentrator_photovoltaics

ABOUT THE AUTHOR

Louis TW Lan grew up and lives in Taiwan. He majored in business administration, and is a master of business administration. He had served in a multinational company and traveled to dozens of countries, learns extensively, likes to improve moral level and spirituality, and has ideals. He hopes to recommend this book to encourage all human beings to abandon the destruction of the earth an all human beings due to greed, hatred and wars leading a further nuclear war, and then work together to achieve "the World of Great Harmony" with love, mutual assistance and happiness!

In addition, in order to achieve the great ideal of "the World of Great Harmony", there must be fair and transparent real estate update on law and taxation to achieve the ideal of "Residents have their own houses". Under the perfect systems, a very small number of organizations and individuals with non-self-use premises are unwilling to hoard non-self-use real estate. Their rights and interests are not compromised.   Existing funds remain unchanged. They just exchange the non-self-use real estate in the metropolitan area into cash, and the funds from the conversion of the real estate into cash are used in other more meaningful ways or investments. The release of many houses/apartments, shops and offices in the metropolitan area will make the price of the premises more reasonable. Those who want to buy self-use houses/apartments, shops and offices in the metropolitan area will be able to purchase them at a more reasonable price. The human ideal of "Residents have their own houses" can be easily and perfectly achieved. The reform of the income tax system does not affect existing funds, but in the future, after "the World of Great Harmony", higher income tax rate will be imposed on a very small number of extremely high-income earners and profiteering individuals/organizations. This higher income tax will be used for the social welfare of all people (from birth to the rebirth of heaven) under "the World of Great Harmony".

The existing funds before "the World of Great Harmony" will remain unchanged. When the "the World of Great Harmony" with love, mutual assistance, and happiness is reached, the social welfare is well conducted and all people are fully taken care of so that future huge income/profit is not needed. I hope that my family will not be harassed and treated unfairly by those who want to continue to have profiteering in "the World of Great Harmony" in the future. Let's love and help each other to live happily and help the earth become "the World of Great Harmony".

This Book is priced at around USD 9.9 and about 80% of net income will be donated to charity. Thank you very much!

Made in the USA
Columbia, SC
04 November 2021

48353453R10065